winning BLACKJACK

T0087921

winning

BLACKJACK

Lyman Hall, Ph.D.

Taylor Trade Publishing

Lanham New York Dallas Boulder Toronto Oxford

Published by Taylor Trade Publishing
An imprint of The Rowman & Littlefield Publishing Group, Inc.
4501 Forbes Boulevard, Suite 200
Lanham, Maryland 20706

Distributed by National Book Network

Library of Congress Cataloging-in-Publication Data

Hall, Lyman, 1935–
    Winning Blackjack / Lyman Hall.—1st Taylor Trade Publishing ed.
        p.   cm.
    ISBN 1-58979-030-8 (pbk.: alk. paper)
    1. Blackjack (Game) 2. Gambling systems. I. Title.

GV1295.B55 H343 2003
795.4'23—dc22   2003016713

∞ The paper used in this publication meets the minimum requirements of American National Standard for Information Sciences—Permanence of Paper for Printed Library Materials, ANSI/NISO Z39.48–1992.

Manufactured in the United States of America.

*Nearly twenty years ago, when I was just
learning the game, I sat next to
my dear friend, Sam Berry, for
a round of blackjack.
I was dealt a 16.
The dealer's up card showed a 7.
Since I was afraid of breaking,
I elected to hold.
The dealer turned over his hole card and
revealed a 10.
I lost.
Sam Berry's "words of comfort" were:
"You deserved to lose."
This pointed observation motivated me
to study the game with intensity.
Thank you, Sam, for pointing me
down the right path.*

CONTENTS

ABOUT LYMAN HALL

Dr. Lyman Hall has been called "America's Dean of Blackjack Teachers." He has played the game in nearly every casino in the United States and Europe. He has also had firsthand experience with offshore casinos in the Caribbean, aboard ships, and on the Internet. In short, he knows how to win in any venue.

In the following pages of *Winning Blackjack*, Dr. Hall gives you his time-tested formula for success. He pulls no punches. He feels your time is too valuable to waste on diplomatic jargon and pie-in-the-sky promises.

Lyman Hall is a product of the academic world. He earned his undergraduate degrees from a small, Midwestern university and graduated with a Ph.D. in communications from Michigan State University. He is familiar with sound teaching techniques. Over the past ten years, he has taught thousands of people how to win at blackjack on a consistent basis.

Using the disciplines of logic and probability, he explains in easy-to-understand language what decisions you should make during a game and why.

In the fact-filled pages of *Winning Blackjack*, Dr. Hall shares with you his insider secrets learned through many years of "trial and terror."

More than just a beginner's bible, *Winning Blackjack* is an indispensable advisor for players at all levels.

Study Dr. Hall's method. Learn his strategies. Follow them to the letter. Then you too can join the legions of satisfied students who enjoy the thrill—not to mention the extra income—they've gained through *Winning Blackjack!*

PREFACE

Welcome to the wonderful world of winning blackjack.

Of all the gaming opportunities at today's casinos, blackjack is the most attractive for serious gamblers. These astute gamers know that blackjack offers the player the best opportunity to control his or her destiny.

Most blackjack players fail to take advantage of this benefit for two reasons:

1. They neglect to follow the proven rules for winning.
2. They program themselves for failure even before the first card is dealt.

I'll elaborate on both subjects later. For now, it's enough to know that this book shows you a system that, *if followed each step of the way*, should give you consistent winnings.

That claim may surprise you. After all, don't most people who visit casinos at one of the nation's gaming capitals or onboard cruise ships confess to losing on a regular basis? Yes, and for good cause. The game is designed to give the house an edge.

Do you think for one minute those gigantic casinos were built because visitors to Las Vegas, Reno, Biloxi, and Atlantic City are winners?

Because the dealer has the luxury of calling for a card only after all other bettors have played, the house has a minimum of a 1.5 percent greater chance of winning. This means that, until now, your chances of winning were 48.5 percent as opposed to the house's 51.5 percent.

This book will show you how you can start turning those odds around beginning with your very next hand.

Is any system perfect? Certainly not. That's why this book contains some guidelines for limiting your losses during those rare times when the cards refuse to fall your way.

At no time will this book mention the term "luck." Luck has no place in a serious bettor's vocabulary. The majority of players fail to understand this. Superstitions abound in the gaming community. Many bettors insist on wearing a certain hat or drinking a favorite beverage while playing blackjack. The famous psychologist B. F. Skinner once referred to this as "an unrelated physical stimulus designed to give a desired response." That's a sophisticated way of saying these things won't help you one bit.

If you want to be a consistent winner, it won't be because of luck, it will be because of skill.

The following pages spell out a ten-rule system for winning blackjack. It has been supported by tests of time and logic. In addition to the ten proven steps to success are some "winner's tips" you'll also want to keep in mind.

For your convenience, there's an easy-to-follow strategy chart on pages 68–69 that tells you what you should do in every situation during a game. There's even another chart on page 72 to help you track your winnings.

Now, get ready to add a dash of fun and excitement to your life through *WINNING BLACKJACK!*

winning BLACKJACK

INTRODUCTION

*It can be argued that man's instinct to gamble
is the only reason he is still not a
monkey up in the trees.*
Mario Puzo

Before you start playing your system, be sure
to review the objectives of blackjack. Although
some of this might seem trite to the veteran
player, a quick review of the fundamental
rules and basic strategies may prove beneficial.

BASIC RULES OF BLACKJACK

Blackjack is a game in which you play against
the dealer. The object of the game is to have
the total point value of your cards greater than
the point value of the dealer's cards without
going over 21. If you go over 21, you "bust,"
even if the dealer goes over 21.

The points for each card equal the numeric value of each card; jacks, queens, and kings count as 10. An ace counts as 1 or 11; you decide which value you wish to apply to your hand.

The dealer gives you two cards. The dealer also receives two cards; one face down, the other face up. Based upon the value of the dealer's "up" card, you determine if you need additional cards. If so, you ask for a "hit." If not, you indicate to the dealer that you will "stand."

On some hands, you might choose to "double down" or to "split pairs." If so, indicate that to the dealer.

To "double down" means that you volunteer to place twice your bet into play. The best time to do this is when you've been dealt cards that total 11 points. Other occasions in which you would be wise to "double" are spelled out in the strategy chart on pages 68–69 of this book.

You may "split" only when you receive two cards of the same kind—two 5s, two 6s, two 7s, and so on. To split means that you place a bet on the table equal to your current bet and create two separate hands to play. Some dealers will even ask you if you want to split. When should you split? One proven rule of thumb is to *always split a pair of 8s*. A point total of 16 is a losing hand. By splitting the 8s, you increase your chances of getting at least one winning hand. Likewise, if you have been dealt two aces, *always split*. You have a good chance of hitting two 21s. Guidelines for splitting also appear on your special strategy chart.

After all players have finished ordering their cards, the dealer turns over the card that is face down. The dealer must draw if his or her hand totals 16 or less or, at some casinos, is a "soft" 17. A "soft" 17 includes an ace and a 6 when the count can equal 7 or 17. If the dealer shows a "hard" 17—a combination of cards that total 17 without benefit of an ace—the dealer must stand.

If the dealer must draw and his or her total is greater than 21, the dealer loses, and all people at the table holding cards with 21 or less points win. If the dealer's final count is between 17 and 21, those at the table with totals greater than that of the dealer (but not higher than 21) are winners. If a player and the dealer end up with the same point total, this is called a "push."

If you are fortunate enough to have been

dealt an ace plus a 10, jack, queen, or king, you have a "blackjack." If so, you receive 1.5 times your wager. The only exception to this is if the dealer also has a blackjack. If so, it's a "push," and you retain your original bet.

Most tables have a minimum bet. Beginning players should bet only at tables with minimum bets of $5 or less. Hit the higher minimum-bet tables later.

Finally, most casinos offer the beginner free instruction at designated times at particular tables. If you're a newcomer to the game, you would be wise to attend one of these training sessions. Remember, however, these casino-sponsored classes show you how to *play* the game; this book shows you how to *win* the game.

Now, let's investigate your winning strategies.

♠ ♥ **WINNER'S TIP** ♦ ♣

Only if you take a personal pledge to follow all ten of these rules can you assure yourself the success for which you are aiming.

TEN RULES FOR WINNING BLACKJACK

Never enter a battle unless the battle is already won before the first shot is fired.
Sun Tsu

RULE #1
FOLLOW THE WINNER'S STRATEGIES OF BETTING

Successful blackjack players *always* follow certain basic strategies of betting. To deviate from them is pure foolishness.

One of the secrets to winning blackjack is to follow certain guidelines as spelled out in detail in the strategy chart on pages 68–69.

Here is the most basic of all strategies. If your cards total 12, 13, 14, 15, or 16, and the card that the dealer has face up is a 7 or higher, *always* take a hit. One of the saddest decisions that novice players make is this: When they have a 16, and the dealer's "up" card is a 7 or higher, they "stand." They surmise that since they are only six points away from breaking, they should take their chances with the cards they have. Poor strategy. Seasoned players anticipate always that the dealer's "down" card is a 10—that's the greatest potential value. Therefore, with a 7 showing, you should anticipate that the dealer has a 17. If so, you have nothing to lose by calling for a "hit" on your 16.

As mentioned earlier, if your cards total 11, *always* double down. If your total is 9, 10, or 11, and the dealer's "up" card is a 3, 4, 5, or 6, *always* double down.

The worst hand you can draw is a 12. In most cases, this is a losing hand from the start.

Here are some rules that winning veterans endorse:

If the dealer is showing a 2, and you have a total of 12, call for one "hit." It matters not what you draw. Then "stand."

One strategy that is debated among even seasoned pros is what you do if you have a total of 12 and the dealer's "up" card is a 3. Some say: "Hit once." Others say: "Stand." Select the option with which you feel the most comfortable. Once you have elected your strategy, stick with it for the remainder of your life. You'll probably end up 50–50 over the span of time.

If you have a 12, and the dealer's "up" card is 4, 5, or 6, *always* "stand."

One final note: If the dealer has an ace as the "up" card, you will be asked if you wish to purchase "insurance," which you may obtain for up to one-half of your original bet. In the event the dealer has a blackjack, you'll be paid double your insurance bet. If the dealer does not have a blackjack, you lose your insurance bet. Experienced players agree: "Insurance is a sucker's bet." Don't take it. In the long run you will lose money.

These are the fundamental rules and strategies of the game of blackjack. Now it's time for you to go to school and learn how you can win *consistently*.

On pages 35–56 of this book are some easy-to-follow examples that tell you when to hit, when to stand, when to split, and when to double down. Follow these rules and increase your chances of winning. If you deviate from these rules, you not only increase your chances of losing, but you also put at risk other players at your table.

If you are a newcomer to blackjack, take the printed guidelines on pages 68–69 with you to the tables. However, to be on the safe side, ask the dealer beforehand if you can refer to them during your game. Most casinos won't mind this as long as you don't share your information with other players at your table. After you've followed these betting strategies for a while, they should become second nature to you, and you will no longer need these printed guidelines.

RULE #2
DOUBLE YOUR BETS FOLLOWING A LOSS

*Chance happens to all, but to turn chance
to account is the gift of few.*
Bulwer-Lytton

This is a fundamental rule of your winning system, yet most blackjack players fail to follow it. In the event that they lose a hand or two, those players continually bet the same amount for each subsequent hand dealt. That's a guaranteed formula for losing.

Here is how this part of your system works:

Let's say your original bet is $5. If you lose a hand, bet $10 on the next deal. If you lose that, bet $20. If you lose that hand, bet $40 on the next deal. As hard as it might be for you to do so, continue the pattern until you win or until you've reached your comfort level. More on this later.

Practice your strategy beginning with a relatively low bet—one, two, or five dollars a hand. That way you won't have to mortgage the home in the event you sustain an unlikely losing streak.

Once you have gained the necessary confidence in your system at the $5 table, you might consider moving up to the $10, $25, or even the $100 table. But, I beg you, take your time. Give yourself a chance to mature in using this system.

I alluded to a rare instance in which you could experience a string of bad hands. Let's say you lose six times in a row. Although the probability of this happening to you is slim, you should prepare yourself for this fate.

That rare streak of bad cards notwithstanding, make a habit of doubling your bets following a loss. In the long run, you will come out ahead.

Some casinos (not many) attempt to prevent players from taking advantage of this strategy by setting a limit on how much they may bet on one hand. A casino, for instance, may limit a $10 table to a $50 bet. If so, you can no longer double your bets after three straight losses. Hence, your odds of winning diminish greatly. Your solution? Change casinos. In all probability, there are plenty of other places just down the street that have no such conservative limits.

If you happen to lose six times in a row, STOP!

On a $5 table, you will have lost a total of $315. Start your system from the beginning with one $5 bet. You'll just have to work a bit longer to regain your losses. Remember the admonition by Kenny Rogers in his popular song: "You gotta know when to hold 'em / know when to fold 'em."

RULE #3
LIMIT YOUR WINS AT EACH TABLE

Bears make money;
bulls make money;
but pigs get slaughtered.
Old Wall Street advice

Most gamers set a limit for *losses*. You are going to do just the opposite. You will set a limit for *wins* at a table.

A key to the success of your winning formula rests in your willingness to win a little at a time, then keep moving.

While sitting at a table, you'll have a streak during which you get great cards at most deals; at other times, you can't seem to buy anything other than 4s or 5s. Likewise, you will discover that the return on your bets will fluctuate up and down. That's the normal pattern in the dealing of cards.

Remember the adage: Quit when you're ahead.

When your wins accumulate to ten to twenty times your original bet, *immediately* cash in your chips and leave the table. That means for a $5 table, you quit after you have won $50 to $100.

Will some players grumble at your interrupting the flow of the game? Possibly. But you're not here to win a popularity contest. You're here to earn a profit.

When I'm playing a $5 table, I set my goal at $100. As soon as I win that amount of money, I leave. You should pick a level with which you are comfortable.

Once you begin to win on a regular basis, you will be tempted to continue playing for hours and hours at a time. That's not a good idea. After several hours of playing (and you'll have to learn your level of endurance through practice), you will become tired. Your mind becomes mushy. You lose concentration. You start making bad bets, and you are setting yourself up for disaster.

Casinos play a psychological trick on us in this regard. In lieu of playing with "real money," they hand out chips. Ever wonder why? As an evening wears on, a $100 chip begins to look and feel the same as a $5 chip. Look at each chip as you would a green bill in your wallet and play accordingly.

If you set a limit for your wins at each table, you should remain alert and can use this system to its full advantage.

Normally, this should take you no more than two or, at the most, three hours of play.

Casinos are well aware of this. They'll attempt to lure you into playing longer with offers such as: "If you play for four hours or more, we'll pay for your hotel room." Avoid that temptation. First, normally casinos give such "comps" only to those who play $25 tables and higher. Second, outside of any "bragging rights" you might gain (e.g., saying to your friends back home that the casino "comped" you), your sloppy play that results from being too tired normally will cost you much more than the money you save on a $50–$100 room.

♠ ♥ WINNER'S TIP ♦ ♣

Limit yourself to a specific amount of winnings for each day. Normally, players at a $5 table who use this system successfully set a goal of earning $300 to $700 a day, then they stop playing blackjack for twenty-four hours.

RULE #4
TREAT THE GAME AS A BUSINESS

*The business of America
is business.*
Calvin Coolidge

"I'm going to bet only $50 tonight; when I lose that, I'll go home." Does this pledge sound all too familiar?

Perhaps you've even said that yourself.

If so, you have set yourself up as a loser. You may as well wear a sign around your neck that reads: "I intend to give to this casino $50 of my money. No questions asked."

From this moment on, vow to treat black-jack playing as a *business*, not as a form of *entertainment*.

Can you, for one minute, imagine an entrepreneur on his or her first day on the job saying to others: "I only intend on losing $50 a day in my new career"? That entrepreneur has probably invested thousands of dollars into establishing a dream. He or she probably was willing to trade the security of a 9-to-5 job for the risky venture of self-employment.

Aware that any new business can have both peaks and valleys, the last thing that entrepreneur needs is a negative attitude that predicts a loss.

Yet, that's exactly the attitude carried by most blackjack players as they enter a casino.

The "I'm-gonna-lose-only-$50" philosophy normally makes a prophet out of the person saying this. This player probably *will* lose the $50. Even before the first card is dealt, the player has set himself or herself up to lose.

You can't afford to do that.

There is an old expression, even among seasoned insiders, that people visit cities such as Las Vegas, Atlantic City, Reno, or Biloxi with the *intention* of losing money. They cite examples of how people sit in front of a slot machine *knowing* they won't leave until they've spent every last quarter or dollar they drop into the slot. Perhaps some people have that feeling. That's not the case, however, with successful blackjack players. They adopt a combatant's attitude, much like the athlete who enters a baseball game or tennis match. They intend to win. They may be visiting a city in order to have fun, certainly, but part of that fun is in winning.

That's what this book is all about.

♠ ♥ **WINNER'S TIP** ♦ ♣

Enter each casino with the realization that you have a winning system and, *if played in its entirety,* **it should earn you profits with each visit.**

RULE #5
LEAVE POOR PLAYERS AT THE TABLE

*I know of no way of judging the future
but by the past.*
Patrick Henry

You're at your favorite casino, playing black-jack and following all the strategies outlined in this book. You're winning on a steady basis, as you should. Suddenly, a newcomer sits at your table. On the next deal, this new player gets cards totaling 16. You are dealt two kings and the dealer shows a 9. Were the new player smart, he would ask for a hit. Instead, he opts to hold. You stay with your 20. The dealer turns over a 5 and draws a 7. Both you and the new player lose. For some unexplained reason, as the deals continue, you get bad cards. Instead of winning on a regular basis, now you're losing.

You become increasingly irritated, especially when you realize that had the new player used the winner's rules, both he and you would have been dealt substantially more winning hands.

And you should be irritated—at two

people. First, you should be disturbed at the neophyte player who entered the game not knowing how to play with sound strategies. Second, you should be angry with yourself for sticking around so long and letting that person ruin your game.

If you observe someone at the table who refuses to abide by the winner's rules for playing, cash in your chips, wish everyone well, then leave the table.

Here's a tactic to use before you sit at a table. Seldom will you find a completely empty table. Especially during the peak hours for gaming, every table will probably have a few players. Before you enter a game, observe the players at the table. If any of the players holds a total of 16 while the dealer's "up" card is 7 or higher, watch how the player reacts. If the player fails to ask for a hit, don't even *think* about sitting at that table. If a player shows poor judgment or lack of knowledge about basic blackjack strategies, don't fool yourself into believing he or she will change. The best prediction of the future is the past. Avoid joining this crowd. There are plenty of other tables in the house.

Once you have determined that all the

other players at the table abide by the winner's strategy of betting, only then should you take a seat.

♠ ♥ WINNER'S TIP ♦ ♣

A big mistake on the part of blackjack players is to assume that choices made by the bad player will not affect your results in the long run because the cards will balance out. Veteran blackjack players know this is not true. History tells us that bad players have a much more negative effect on you. Leave the table. Let those poor players irritate someone else.

RULE #6
SIT AT THIRD BASE

*When calling a play, of more importance
than being close to the action
is having the best possible angle.*
Umpire Harry Wendelstedt

For those who are unfamiliar with this term, "third base" is the designation for the last position at the table that is dealt cards. Cards are dealt in a clockwise rotation. Therefore, the person sitting to the farthest left of the dealer receives his or her cards first. The rest of the players receive theirs in turn.

The person playing third base is the last one to receive a card prior to the dealer. That person is the most influential in controlling the game. In short, the person sitting at third base can make or break a hand for the entire table depending on his or her choice to draw or to stand. In order to help guarantee your success at the table, make certain that YOU are the one occupying that third-base position.

What if the person already playing third

base appears to be a good player? Don't be fooled by that false sense of security. I have seen many instances in which players follow the rules as presented in this book for as much as a half-hour or so. Suddenly, and without warning, they start playing dumb.

The only way to prevent this from happening to you is for you to occupy that place.

There is one further advantage to playing third base. Because you are the last person receiving cards, you have a bit more time in order to think of your situation and to plan your strategy. Outside of playing while intoxicated, the most dangerous position into which you can place yourself at the blackjack table is to join the game while you feel pressured to make a quick decision.

♠ ♥ **WINNER'S TIP** ♦ ♣

Always play a game sitting at third base. If the third-base slot at a table is occupied, wait for the player to leave. Do not play unless you are sitting at third base.

RULE #7
WEIGH THE DECK

*A wise man sees as much as he ought,
not as much as he can.*
Montaigne

This rule works effectively only at a table at which a dealer uses *only one or two decks*. It should *not* be used at a table using a six- or eight-deck "shoe."

Every seasoned blackjack player knows that after the first deal, the remaining deck has a "weight." High cards—10 through ace—are considered "heavy." Low cards—2 through 6—are "light." Cards that are 7, 8, or 9 are "neutral."

Observe the cards dealt on the first hand. If there is a predominance of small cards dealt, that means the deck contains a greater percentage of high cards. The remaining deck, therefore, is "heavy." Conversely, if more large cards are distributed during the first deal, the remaining deck contains a higher percentage of small cards. That deck is "light."

Without going into the mathematical formula to explain this, it's enough for you to remember that a "heavy" deck favors the player; a "lighter" deck favors the dealer.

If, on the first deal, the deal shows six more low cards than high cards, double your next bet. Your chance of winning has now increased to about 55 percent. If, on the other hand, you notice six more large cards dealt than low cards, sit out a hand or two until the deck becomes more balanced.

♠ ♥ WINNER'S TIP ♦ ♣

Most casinos have a policy of barring so-called "card counters" from playing on their property. Therefore, if you are playing at a one- or two-deck table and notice six or seven more low cards dealt, don't announce to everyone else playing that their percentage for winning has sharply increased. Instead, quietly double your bet. Even if the dealer or pit boss knows what you are doing, chances are they will not question you if you just keep your strategy to yourself.

RULE #8
DON'T TALK AT THE TABLE

*Don't speak unless you can
improve the silence.*
Unknown

Another key to winning blackjack is your
ability to concentrate on your cards and those
dealt to other players. This is not the time to
socialize. Conversations with others only
interfere with your focus.

This is especially true with the dealer. The
dealer has one objective: to take your money.
Each dealer answers to a pit boss who keeps
an eagle eye on his or her table. If a dealer
loses too many hands, that dealer may be
asked to sit down. If a dealer is known to lose
money for the house on a continual basis, that
dealer is destined to join the ranks of the
unemployed.

Some dealers are genuinely friendly. They
have no qualms about interrupting your concentration with innocent queries such as:
"How are you?" or "Where are you from?"

My advice when this happens to you:

Silently nod, smile, look away, then place your wager. Normally the dealer will realize you wish not to talk and will honor your choice.

If you feel you *must* talk to the dealer on occasion, wait until the dealer shuffles the cards. It's OK at this time to engage in some friendly dialogue. It may even ease tension you have built from concentration. Once your next hand is dealt, however, it's time to keep quiet.

The rule against talking while at the table also includes those who come to the casino with you. Often your spouse or another friend will stand behind you as you're playing and comment on how well you're playing or ask how long you intend to play. Conversations with these folks can also add to the interruption of your concentration.

An effective strategy for you that not only will help you in your game but will also assist in preserving good relationships is to explain to your companion that once you sit at the table, you do not talk. Explain why. Once your companion understands, you should have no further problem.

If your dealer insists on gabbing with you while you are concentrating on your cards, politely tell him or her that you would rather not talk while playing. If the dealer keeps talking, either notify the pit boss or cash in your chips and move on.

RULE #9
NEVER DRINK WHILE PLAYING

Drunkenness is temporary suicide.
Bertrand Russell

Have you ever wondered why casinos often make a habit of serving free alcoholic drinks to gamblers? Is it because the casino owners are just "good guys" who want to make you feel at home? Serious blackjack players know there's a more logical explanation.

Casino owners realize that alcohol consumption creates dull minds. Dull minds make poorer bets. Poorer bets result in losing hands. Losing hands build those big casinos.

In fact, it's good practice to avoid drinking *any* beverage while playing. Simply reaching for a cup of coffee or a soft drink can break your concentration.

Along this same line, avoid playing the game when you are physically, mentally, or emotionally drained. For example, if you are sleepy from a long flight, if you are rushed to catch another plane, if you're hungry, or if you have just had a fight with your spouse or significant other, save your blackjack play for another time. If you *insist* on gambling, visit a nearby slot machine at which concentration is not essential.

♠ ♥ WINNER'S TIP ♦ ♣

If a cocktail waitress stops by and asks if you want anything to drink, don't even respond. Stare at your cards. Concentrate on the game. She'll not get angry with you, but will move on. Chances are she will not bother you again.

RULE #10
PRACTICE AND PRACTICE, AND THEN PRACTICE SOME MORE

*Genius is one percent inspiration and
ninety-nine percent perspiration.*
Thomas Edison

The late Henny Youngman often repeated a classic story in his comedy routines: "A man carrying a violin under his arm approaches a stranger along New York's Fifth Avenue and asks, 'How do I get to Carnegie Hall?' The stranger responds, 'Practice, man. Practice.'"

The same sage advice applies to you as a blackjack player, just as it does in every other discipline.

Have you ever noticed how superstars of sport make the skills of the game appear easy? But do you think for one minute that the late baseball great Ted Williams developed his smooth swing overnight? Was Johnny Unitas born with the ability to throw pinpoint passes in the National Football League? Did Tiger

Woods break par in his first round of golf? Each of these pros devoted long hours to honing their skills.

So should you.

By practicing your newfound strategies, you'll gain confidence in your ability to apply them. That's important. Unless you have confidence in yourself, you'll not have confidence in your game.

One way to practice your *Winning Blackjack* skills is to visit a local computer store and purchase a game that simulates blackjack. Another way to practice is to find a deck of cards lying around your house. Play the roles of both dealer and player. Whatever tool you use, practice using the strategies learned in this book so they become second nature to you.

Your effectiveness will be directly related to how much you practice. When you play in a real game, you should be able to make decisions instantly. There will be no reason to ponder.

To the outsider, you'll make playing the game look so smooth and easy. Who knows?

They might even call you the "Ted Williams of blackjack."

♠ ♥ WINNER'S TIP ♦ ♣

Start slowly. Once you've mastered your winning blackjack strategies, only then should you step into the arena of real-world blackjack. If you can find one, start at a $1 table. If you make a mistake or two, you won't be hurt too badly. As you gain confidence, move on up.

A QUICK REVIEW OF YOUR STRATEGIES FOR WINNING BLACKJACK

If winning isn't important,
why do they keep score?
Orel Hershiser

1. Follow the winner's strategies of betting. Each rule is here for a purpose—to increase your odds of winning.

2. Double your bets following a loss. Through simple mathematics, you can prove that you should win in the long run.

3. Limit your wins at each table. Once you have earned ten or twenty times your initial bet, cash in your chips and move on.

4. Treat the game as a business. Sure, you're there to have fun, but it's much *more* fun when you're winning.

5. Leave poor players at the table. Over the course

of time, these people will hurt your chances of winning.

6. Sit at third base. This is the best position for you to control the game and to have a little extra time to plan your strategy.

7. Weigh the deck. This observation regarding "heavy" cards and "light" cards should help you in a one- or two-deck deal.

8. Don't talk at the table. Keep your socializing for the times before or after the game.

9. Never drink while playing. Drinking any beverage serves only as a distraction. You don't need this.

10. Practice and practice, and then practice some more. Your key to success is in direct relationship to the amount of time you practice your play.

Okay, now that you are comfortable with your system for winning blackjack, let's put into practice some of the strategies you've learned along the way.

Following are ten common situations in which you will find yourself over the next few years. In each case, you'll have to make a decision as to what will work best for you.

On the facing page of each situation posed by two photographs, you will find the best guide for you. In addition, I give you the rationale behind the proper choice.

Remember, please, that no one response to a specific situation will work in your favor 100 percent of the time. Instead, as has been the premise held throughout this book, these are the choices that will benefit you more often than not.

Are you ready to test yourself? If so, let's give it a try.

The dealer shows:

You hold:

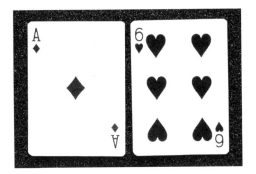

You should hit.

Although you are holding a "soft 17"—two or more cards that total 17 because of the ace, which can count either as 1 or 11—you probably have a losing hand. Here's why.

You must always assume that the dealer's down card is a 10, because that's the card value the dealer is more apt to have as the down card. If this is the case, the dealer ends up with a total of 18, and you lose.

Therefore, you should hit and hope to hit for a 2, 3, or 4.

If you draw a 10 and end up with a "hard 17," then you stay and hope the dealer's down card turns up anything except a card valued at 10 or 11. If you draw a 9 or less, hit again until your total reaches a number from 17 to 21.

The dealer shows:

You hold:

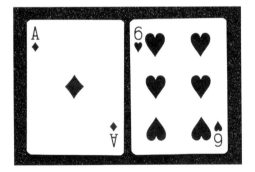

You should double.

A 6 is the worst card any dealer (or any player) can draw. It presents the greatest potential for a "break hand"—one that is greater than 21. For you, in this situation, a 17 may be a winning hand, but the dealer is vulnerable. By doubling and taking one card, you have an excellent chance for collecting two times your original bet.

The dealer shows:

You hold:

You should split.

In fact, you *always* split 8s. Two 8s equal 16. That's a losing hand.

No matter what the dealer shows, your chances of getting at least one winning hand out of the remaining cards that are dealt are good enough that you'll, at least, get back your original bet.

The dealer shows:

You hold:

You should double.

Always double if your first two cards total 11—even if the dealer's "up" card is an ace.

That dealer's ace may look intimidating, and you might fear he or she is sitting on a blackjack. Not so. If he or she had a blackjack, the dealer would be compelled to reveal this prior to any wagering after your original bet.

The dealer shows:

You hold:

You should stand.

Some neophyte players view two face cards as an opportunity to split; they hope for twice the winnings against the dealer's relatively horrible 5 card. Don't even *think* about splitting face cards or 10s.

A 5 card is an indication that the dealer will break, certainly. But your 20 is an extremely strong hand. In this instance, it's an almost sure winner. Therefore, keep your hand and count your blessings.

The dealer shows:

You hold:

You should split.

You may be tempted to hold onto your total of 8 and hope to receive a 10 as your next card, but that would give you a total of 18. Veteran blackjack players agree: An 18 is a weak hand. They feel much more comfortable with cards totaling 19, 20, or 21.

In this situation, even if you fall short of gaining a total of 17 on each of the hands begun with the 4s, you shouldn't have many anxieties. After all, with a 6, the dealer has a good chance of breaking.

By the way, you should apply this same strategy each time you hold the same cards and the dealer shows a 4 or a 5.

The dealer shows:

You hold:

You should hit.

Although the dealer shows a less-than-ideal hand, and you may be tempted to split your pair of 4s, follow the rules of probability and hit.

The dealer's 3 presents too many possibilities for the dealer eventually to draw cards that total 17–21. Had you elected to split your cards, you would start each of two hands with a 4. It's enough of a statistical disadvantage that you would be better off by asking for a hit. When you do, if your first card brings your count to 11 or less, ask for one more hit until your total reaches 12–21, then stop. You've played the best you can.

The dealer shows:

You hold:

You should stand.

As mentioned earlier, an 18 is not a potent hand. In this instance, it may well be all you need in order to win.

Remember the basic rule: Always consider the dealer's down card to be worth 10. If so, your 18 *is* a winning hand.

You might be tempted to split your 9s since you might draw 10s. Indeed you might. But, in order for you to profit from your strategy, you must do this twice. That's stretching your luck. Go with the percentages and stand.

The dealer shows:

You hold:

You should hit.

The most misunderstood hand by beginning blackjack players is an ace and a 7. This "soft 18," on the surface, appears to be a winning hand. In reality, it's a loser.

This makes much more sense once you realize that the average dealer's hand totals 18.5. It doesn't take a rocket scientist to realize that, in the long run, you will win more money if you aim for a total of 19, 20, or 21.

Were you to hold a "hard 18," of course, you would stand and hope that the dealer reveals his or her down card (often called a "hole card") to be less than an ace or a 10.

The dealer shows:

You hold:

You should "surrender."

All right, I know this option has not been covered in this book, nor is it mentioned on your strategy chart at the end. The reason for the omission of this concept so far in this book is that most of today's casinos will not accept this option. Consider, then, this subject of "surrender" as your first class in "graduate school" of blackjack playing.

A "surrender" is the voluntary admission on your part that you have a horrible hand after your first two cards are dealt, especially as compared to the potential of the dealer's 10. By surrendering, you give up half of your original bet and cease playing until the next deal.

Nobody likes to lose money—especially without a fight. But, in this instance, you are merely attempting to cut back on your losses.

If the casino permits you to do so, you should surrender when:

- Your first two cards total 15, and the dealer shows a 10.
- Your first two cards total 16, and the dealer shows a 9, 10, or ace.

There are no hand signals for "surrender," therefore you must tell the dealer that you want to surrender when it's your turn to act on your cards.

MANAGING YOUR BANK

*It's not a matter of how much money you earn,
rather it's a matter of how much
money you keep.*
J. P. Morgan

Most novice players fail to realize that when playing blackjack, they must create and manage a personal bank. Similar to those stately buildings in their hometowns, these banks follow much of the same philosophy in terms of calculated risks, profit-to-debt ratio, credit line, sound investments, and management.

Immediately after you sit at a table (hopefully at third base), even before the first card is dealt, you will create your bank. First, you hand the dealer some hard cash that is converted into chips. This is your "active account." In addition, you'll store extra money in your pocket that you may have to use as the game progresses. This is called your "reserve."

How you parlay the two can mean the difference between success and failure in your *Winning Blackjack* results.

Here's a way in which I have used this bank to work for me over the past few decades. You may wish to adopt your own comfort zone, but this should get you started in terms of a workable plan.

I'll establish my "active account" in the amount of twenty times my original bet. If I'm at a $5 table, I convert $100 into chips. If I'm at a $10 table, that amount increases to $200. At the same time, in my pocket, I'll keep a bit more than two times the amount I've invested. For every $100 in my "active account," I keep $215 in my pocket as my "reserve." No more. No less.

If the first few hands go as they should, you'll have no need to dip into your reserve. Instead, you'll amass enough winnings along the way to increase your pile of chips. If, on the other hand, you start off with a series of, let's say, five losses in a row (it's rare, but it can happen), and if you double your bets following a loss as discussed in Rule #2, you will have to dip into your reserve.

How often should you double? Here's where your management skills come into play. If I lose six times in a row, I have lost a total of $315 (hence the suggested amount of money you should keep in your pocket as your "reserve"). I then leave the table and start elsewhere.

The reason behind this rather conservative approach is this: If I have lost six times in a row, then I must invest another $320 in order to gain just a $5 profit overall. To me, that's not good stewardship. My comfort level tells me that a total of $315 is all I wish to invest.

Also, it's just sound banking practice.

A PERSONAL NOTE FROM THE AUTHOR

Today's modern casinos overflow with symbols of luxury and success. Handpainted ceilings, elegant statues, crystal chandeliers, polished marble floors—all provide appropriate settings for visitors who sport the latest designer fashions. All this glitz, glitter, and pompous display of wealth may lead us to conclude that everyone associated with the industry is rolling in money.

Not so. A lot of casino employees work long hours for little more than high school students working at a part-time job. One such employee stands across the table from you dealing cards.

Your dealer must make mortgage payments like everyone else. He or she must save money to send kids to college. These are challenging ambitions for people earning a base salary approaching minimum wage. The only way for a dealer to earn a respectable salary is through tips.

Question: Should you tip your dealer?

Answer: Sure. Why not?

At the close of a successful run at the table, I see nothing wrong with giving a dealer a tip in the amount of my original bet.

However, some players lose money unnecessarily by tipping the dealer *during* the game. They feel that, by some mystical intervention, the gods of blackjack will somehow turn their cards into winning hands. Bah! Save that sort of thinking for the next *Harry Potter* book.

Follow the rules outlined in this book. Remember your friendly dealer. And, above all, enjoy your newfound success at the world's greatest game.

In the meantime, if you see me at any of the casinos, stop by and introduce yourself. I'm easy to find. I'll be playing third base.

—**Lyman Hall**

GLOSSARY OF BLACKJACK TERMS

Anchor: *See* "Third Base."

Barring a Player: The act of a casino refusing to allow a player (normally a card counter) from participating in any more games at that venue.

Break a Deck: *See* "Shuffle."

Burn a Card: The term used when a dealer takes away the top card from a deck and places it, unseen, in a separate plastic case used to hold dealt cards.

Bust: To call for a hit and the total reaches more than 21, thus creating a losing hand.

Bust Card: A name given to a 2, 3, 4, 5, or 6 as the dealer's "up" card.

Bust Hand: A name given when a hand totals

12–16 and puts the hand in danger of surpassing a total of 21 on the next draw.

Card Counter: The designation for someone who keeps track of the cards played in order to determine whether or not the remaining cards in the deck are favorable.

Double Down: The choice of a player to double an original bet. Normally a player indicates this by turning over both cards and adding the amount of the original wager alongside the cards.

First Baseman: The name given to the first person dealt cards. Many experts claim this is the second-best seat in the house for you.

Hit: To add a card to your dealt hand.

Hole Card: The name given to the dealer's face-down card in the deal.

Insurance: An option provided by the dealer that allows a player to wager half of an original bet when the dealer's "up" card is an ace.

Natural: The combination of an ace and a card worth 10 dealt as the first two cards, thus producing a blackjack.

Shoe: A box containing normally six or eight decks of cards used for dealing in most of today's casinos.

Shuffle: To divide the deck into halves (splitting the deck) several times, then mixing them prior to a deal.

Single-Deck Game: A deal in which the dealer holds only one deck of cards. Many veteran players feel this type of game holds an advantage for them.

Soft Hand: The term given when a player elects to count an ace as an 11. For example, when holding an ace and a 6, the player regards the total as a "soft" 17.

Splitting Pairs: An option that allows a player to separate cards of equal value into the start of two separate hands. If a player is dealt two 10-value cards, he or she may split these as well, although this is not considered good strategy.

Stand: Refuse to accept another hit from the dealer.

Stiff Hand: A hand totaling 12–16 that is vulnerable to busting with one draw.

Ten-Value Card: A 10, jack, queen, or king that is counted as 10 toward the total of a deal given to a player or dealer.

Third Base: Term given to the last seat at the table; the player in third base gets his or her cards last. This player, sometimes called the "anchor," is the one who has the greatest impact on the game.

Up Card: One of the first two cards given to the dealer, which is face up.

LYMAN HALL'S STRATEGY CHART

YOUR HAND	DEALER'S "UP" CARD									
	2	3	4	5	6	7	8	9	10	A
17–21	S	S	S	S	S	S	S	S	S	S
16	S	S	S	S	S	H	H	H	H	H
15	S	S	S	S	S	H	H	H	H	H
14	S	S	S	S	S	H	H	H	H	H
13	S	S	S	S	S	H	H	H	H	H
12	H	S/H	S	S	S	H	H	H	H	H
11	D	D	D	D	D	D	D	D	D	D
10	D	D	D	D	D	D	D	D	H	H
9	H	D	D	D	D	H	H	H	H	H
8	H	H	H	H	H	H	H	H	H	H
7	H	H	H	H	H	H	H	H	H	H
6	H	H	H	H	H	H	H	H	H	H
5	H	H	H	H	H	H	H	H	H	H

A, 9	S	S	S	S	S	S	S	S	S	S
A, 8	S	S	S	S	D	S	S	S	S	S
A, 7	S	D	D	D	D	S	S	H	H	H
A, 6	H	D	D	D	D	H	H	H	H	H
A, 5	H	H	D	D	D	H	H	H	H	H
A, 4	H	H	D	D	D	H	H	H	H	H
A, 3	H	H	H	D	D	H	H	H	H	H
A, 2	H	H	H	D	D	H	H	H	H	H
A, A	Sp	Sp	Sp	Sp	Sp	Sp	Sp	Sp	Sp	Sp
2, 2/3, 3/4, 4	Sp	Sp	Sp	Sp	Sp	Sp	H	H	H	H
5, 5	D	D	D	D	D	D	D	D	H	H
6, 6	Sp	Sp	Sp	Sp	Sp	H	H	H	H	H
7, 7	Sp	Sp	Sp	Sp	Sp	Sp	H	H	H	H
8, 8	Sp	Sp	Sp	Sp	Sp	Sp	Sp	Sp	Sp	Sp
9, 9	Sp	Sp	Sp	Sp	Sp	S	Sp	Sp	S	S

H = Hit   S = Stand   D = Double Down   Sp = Split

YOUR RECORD OF WINNINGS

Lynn Balaban, C.P.A. for the firm of Balaban and Schmidt, P.A., in Daytona Beach, Florida, reminds us that IRS Code 165(d) requires us to report all gaming income as "miscellaneous income"—including our winnings from blackjack. These winnings, however, may be offset by any losses at the table known as "wagering losses" (which, if you employ all the strategies in this book, should be few), which are deductible on "Schedule A."

Here is a convenient chart for your records that will show exactly how much money you have pocketed from your playing skills throughout a calendar year. It's the sort of record required by the IRS and one that should help reinforce for you the powerful results of your strategies for *Winning Blackjack!*

Date	Casino	Amount Wagered	Amount Netted (+ or −)	Remarks

SUGGESTED READING

The serious blackjack player is always a student. Repeated winners of the game testify that every time they read a new book about the game, they learn something valuable—something that has helped them earn extra money.

The following is a selected list of books currently in print. For each book, I have included the title, the names of the author and publisher, plus the year it came into print. You may find these at your neighborhood bookstore, at gift shops in casinos, or on the Internet using one or more of the popular websites available.

Happy reading.

Anderson, Ian, *Burning the Tables in Las Vegas* (Huntington Press, 1999)

Benson, Michael, and Sugar, Bert, *Blackjack Strategy* (The Lyons Press, 2000)

Canfield, Richard, *Blackjack: Your Way to Riches* (Lyle Stuart, 1989)

Carlson, Bruce, *Blackjack for Blood* (Gamestar, 2000)

Cromwell, Gordon, *Win at Blackjack* (Oldcastle Books, Ltd., 1990)

Ford, Roger, *Advantage Blackjack* (Silverthorne Publications, 1999)

Gollehon, *All about Blackjack* (Perigee, 1987)

Griffin, Peter, *Theory of Blackjack* (Huntington Press, 1999)

Harvey, Richard, *Blackjack the Smart Way* (Mystic Ridge Productions, 1999)

Harvey, Richard, *Blackjack the Smart Way, The Millennium Edition* (Mystic Ridge Productions, 2000)

Marshall, Angie, *A Woman's Guide to Blackjack* (Lyle Stuart, 1999)

May, John, *Get the Edge at Blackjack* (Bonus Books, 2000)

Pappadopoulos, George, *Blackjack's Hidden Secrets* (ME-n-U Marketers, 2000)

Renzey, Fred, *Blackjack Bluebook* (Blackjack Mentor, 1997)

Revere, Lawrence, *Playing Blackjack as a Business* (Lyle Stuart, 1977)

Schlesinger, Don, *Blackjack Attack* (RGE Publishing, 2000)

Scoblete, Frank, *Best Blackjack* (Bonus Books, 1996)

Scott, Frank, *Blackjack for Winners* (Barricade Books, 1993)

Snyder, Arnold, *Blackjack Wisdom* (RGE Publishing, 1997)

Thomason, Walter, *Blackjack for the Clueless* (Lyle Stuart, 1998)

Thomason, Walter, *Twenty-First Century Blackjack* (Bonus Books, 1999)

Throp, Edward, *Beat the Dealer* (Random House, 1966)

Uston, Ken, and Roberts, Stanley, *Million Dollar Blackjack* (Carol Publishers, 1992)

Vancura, Olaf, and Fuchs, Ken, *Knock-Out Blackjack* (Huntington Press, 1998)

Wong, Stanford, *Basic Blackjack* (Pi Yee Press, 1992)

INDEX